AMAZING
BASKETBALL
RECORDS

BY THOM STORDEN

WITHDRAWN

Reading Consultant:
Barbara J. Fox
Professor Emerita
North Carolina State University

CAPSTONE PRESS
a capstone imprint

Blazers Books are published by Capstone Press,
1710 Roe Crest Drive, North Mankato, Minnesota 56003
www.capstonepub.com

Library of Congress Cataloging-in-Publication Data
Storden, Thom.
Amazing basketball records / by Thom Storden
pages cm.—(Blazers Books. Epic sports records.)
Includes bibliographical references and index.
Summary: "Provides information on the most stunning records in the sport of professional
basketball"—Provided by publisher.
Audience: Age: 8-14.
Audience: Grade: 4 to 6.
ISBN 978-1-4914-0741-7 (library binding)
ISBN 978-1-4914-0746-2 (eBook PDF)
1. Basketball—Records—Juvenile literature. I. Title.
GV885.45.S76 2015
796.323—dc23

2014008655

Editorial Credits
Nate LeBoutillier, editor; Kyle Grenz, designer; Eric Gohl, media researcher;
Kathy McColley, production specialist

Photo Credits
AP Photo: Chris Carlson, cover (top), Eric Gay, cover (bottom), 9, Paul Vathis, 7; Getty Images: NBAE/
Andrew D. Bernstein, 27, NBAE/Dick Raphael, 13, NBAE/Nathaniel S. Butler, 15, NBAE/Neil Leifer,
28, Robert Riger, 17; Newscom: Agence France Presse/Brian Bahr, 20, Agence France Presse/Jeff
Haynes, 23, Icon SMI/John McDonough, 10, Icon SMI/Sporting News Archives, 5, Icon SMI/TSN, 19,
KRT/Gary Bogdon, 24; Shutterstock: Gary Paul Lewis, 2–3, Torsak Thammachote, 1, 30–31, 32
Design Elements: Shuttestock

Records in this book are current through the 2013–14 season.

Printed in in the United States of America in Stevens Point, Wisconsin.
032014   008092WZF14

TABLE OF
CONTENTS

HOW DO WE
MEASURE AMAZING?. 4

INDIVIDUAL RECORDS. 6

TEAM RECORDS. 14

POSTSEASON RECORDS. . . .18

CAN YOU
BELIEVE IT? RECORDS. . . . 24

Glossary 30
Read More 31
Internet Sites 31
Index 32

HOW DO WE MEASURE AMAZING?

Basketball is a very **competitive** sport. How do we appreciate great performances yet separate the best from the rest? How do we transform glorious moments in time into golden memories? Keeping records is one way to do it.

competitive–trying to be the best

EPIC//FACT

Bill Russell won 11 National Basketball Association (NBA) championships, more than any other player.

BILL RUSSELL

MOST POINTS IN ONE GAME 100

The game where Wilt Chamberlain scored 100 points was unusual. The opponents began to foul Chamberlain's teammates to keep him from scoring. Chamberlain's teammates then fouled to stop the clock. With just 46 seconds left, Chamberlain scored his 100th point.

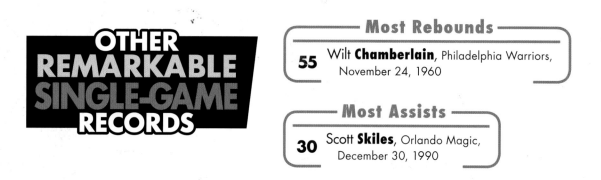

OTHER REMARKABLE SINGLE-GAME RECORDS

Most Rebounds

55 Wilt **Chamberlain**, Philadelphia Warriors, November 24, 1960

Most Assists

30 Scott **Skiles**, Orlando Magic, December 30, 1990

EPIC//FACT

WILT CHAMBERLAIN

7

MOST THREE-POINTERS IN A SEASON 272

Stephen Curry was born to shoot a basketball. His father, Dell, played 16 seasons in the pros and made 1,245 three-pointers. In the 2012–13 season, Stephen sank 272 three-pointers. Setting this record must have made his father proud.

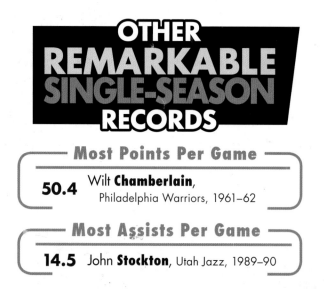

OTHER REMARKABLE SINGLE-SEASON RECORDS

Most Points Per Game

50.4 Wilt **Chamberlain**, Philadelphia Warriors, 1961–62

Most Assists Per Game

14.5 John **Stockton**, Utah Jazz, 1989–90

EPIC//FACT

Stephen Curry's younger brother, Seth, made his first pro appearance with the Memphis Grizzlies in 2014.

EPIC//FACT

Kareem Abdul-Jabbar was born Lew Alcindor. He changed his name at age 24.

KAREEM ABDUL-JABBAR

MOST POINTS ALL TIME
38,387

No one put the ball in the basket like Kareem Abdul-Jabbar. The towering center had an unstoppable shot called The Skyhook. He released it with one hand from behind his head in a sweeping motion. No one could block it.

OTHER INDIVIDUAL CAREER RECORDS

Most Games Played
1,611   Robert **Parish**
four teams

Most Blocks
3,830   Hakeem **Olajuwon**
Houston Rockets, Toronto Raptors

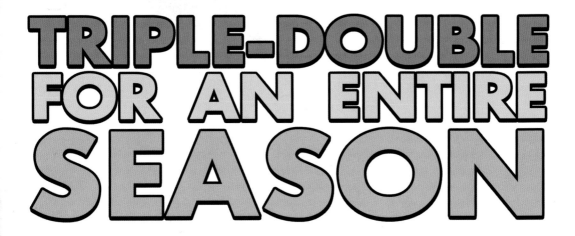

TRIPLE-DOUBLE FOR AN ENTIRE SEASON

Achieving a **triple-double** shows great all-around ability. Oscar Robertson is the only player ever to average a triple-double over an entire season. In the 1961–62 season, "The Big O" averaged 30.8 points, 12.5 rebounds, and 11.4 assists per game.

> **triple-double**—a feat where, in a single game, a player achieves double figures in three different areas, such as points, rebounds, and assists

EPIC//FACT

Oscar Robertson was the NBA's all-time assist leader when he retired in 1974.

OSCAR ROBERTSON

BEST RECORD IN A SEASON 72-10

Teams who played the charging Chicago Bulls in the 1995–96 season were often trampled. Michael Jordan scored. Scottie Pippen played great defense. Dennis Rodman rebounded. The rest of the Bulls were excellent **complementary** players. Their 72 regular season wins is an all-time high.

OTHER REMARKABLE TEAM RECORDS

Best Home Record
40-1 **Boston Celtics**, 1985–86

Best Road Record
31-7 **Los Angeles Lakers**, 1971–72

complementary–adding what is needed to make something successful

EPIC//FACT

The Bulls won the NBA championship six times in the 1990s.

MICHAEL JORDAN

SCOTTIE PIPPEN

DENNIS RODMAN

MOST CHAMPIONSHIPS WON 17

No pro basketball team has had more success than the Boston Celtics. They have won 17 titles. But the Celtics were especially terrific in the 1960s. They won 9 titles in 10 years. The Los Angeles Lakers were the runners-up for 6 of those titles.

EPIC//FACT

HIGHEST POINTS-PER-GAME AVERAGE 46.3

Los Angeles Lakers guard Jerry West was also known as "Mr. **Clutch**." West was at his best in a playoff series against the Baltimore Bullets in 1965. He averaged an amazing 46.3 points per game.

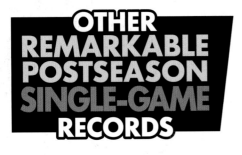

OTHER REMARKABLE POSTSEASON SINGLE-GAME RECORDS

Most Points in a **Postseason Game**

63 Michael **Jordan**, Chicago Bulls
versus Boston Celtics, April 20, 1986

Most Rebounds in a **Postseason Game**

41 Wilt **Chamberlain**, Philadelphia 76ers
versus Boston Celtics, April 5, 1967

clutch—able to perform one's best in the most important games or situations

18

JERRY WEST

EPIC//FACT

Jerry West was voted to the
All-Star team in each one of
his 14 pro seasons.

MICHAEL JORDAN

EPIC//FACT

Michael Jordan quit basketball
to play minor league baseball
in 1994. He returned to playing
basketball in 1995.

MOST CAREER POINTS IN POSTSEASON PLAY 5,987

When Michael "Air" Jordan had the ball in his hands, fans knew that the ball would soon be in the hoop. The only question was, "How?" For years Jordan entertained fans answering that question. He scored more points in the playoffs than any other player.

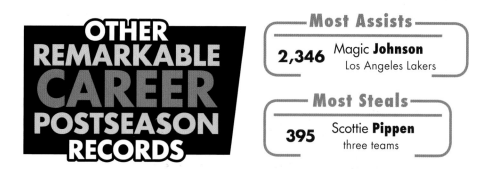

OTHER REMARKABLE CAREER POSTSEASON RECORDS

Most Assists

2,346   Magic **Johnson**
       Los Angeles Lakers

Most Steals

395   Scottie **Pippen**
     three teams

MOST CHAMPIONSHIPS WON BY A COACH 11

As a player Phil Jackson's skills were average. What made him valuable, though, was that he was hardworking, thoughtful, and **scrappy**. These same qualities made him a great coach. Jackson was known for **motivating** some of the greatest players to do their best.

scrappy—full of a fighting spirit

motivate—to encourage someone to do something

EPIC//FACT

PHIL JACKSON

KOBE
BRYANT

EPIC//FACT

Kobe Bryant scored 18 points
in his first All-Star game.

YOUNGEST AGE TO PLAY IN THE ALL-STAR GAME 19

Kobe Bryant played in the pros the same year he graduated high school. The next season, at age 19, he made the All-Star team. Kobe had success early in his career. At age 21 he won his first championship with the Los Angeles Lakers.

OTHER REMARKABLE RECORDS

Youngest Player to Play a Game

18 years, **6** days — Andrew **Bynum**, Los Angeles Lakers, 2005

Oldest Player to Play a Game

45 years, **363** days — Nat **Hickey**, Providence Steam Rollers, 1948

MOST SHOTS WITHOUT A MAKE IN A GAME 17

Some days the ball just doesn't go in the hoop. For Tim Hardaway, December 28, 1991, was one of those days. Hardaway shot the ball 17 times during the game, but not a single shot went in. Luckily, he had 13 assists, and his team still won the game.

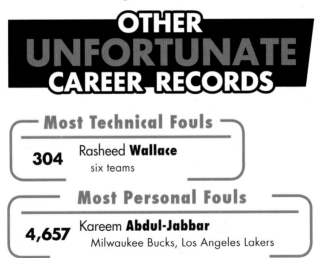

OTHER UNFORTUNATE CAREER RECORDS

Most Technical Fouls

304 Rasheed **Wallace**
six teams

Most Personal Fouls

4,657 Kareem **Abdul-Jabbar**
Milwaukee Bucks, Los Angeles Lakers

TIM HARDAWAY

EPIC//FACT

Tim Hardaway made the All-Star
team 5 times in his 15 pro seasons.

NATE ARCHIBALD

EPIC//FACT

Nate Archibald was the starting point guard for the 1980–81 NBA Champion Boston Celtics.

THE ONE AND ONLY

Nate "Tiny" Archibald of the Kansas City-Omaha Kings led the league in both scoring and passing in the 1972–73 season. He averaged an amazing 34 points and 11.4 assists per game. Tiny remains the only NBA player to have achieved this feat.

ONLY PLAYER TO...

Average 50 Points in a Single Season
Wilt **Chamberlain**, Philadelphia Warriors
50.4 points per game, 1960–61

Play at Least 1,000 Straight Games
A.C. **Green**, four teams from 1986–2001
played 1,192 straight games

GLOSSARY

clutch (KLUHCH)—able to perform one's best in the most important games or situations

competitive (kum-PET-i-tiv)—trying to be the best

complementary (kom-pluh-MEN-tuh-ree)—adding what is needed to make something successful

motivate (MOH-tuh-vayt)—to encourage someone to do something

scrappy (SKRAP-ee)—full of a fighting spirit

triple-double (TRIP-uhl-DUB-uhl)—a feat in basketball where, in a single game, a player achieves double figures in three different areas, such as points, rebounds, and assists

READ MORE

Levit, Joseph, Tim Gramling, Steven Bennett, and Zachary Cohen. *Sports Illustrated Kids STATS!* New York: Time Home Entertainment, Inc., 2013.

LeBoutillier, Nate. *The Best of Everything Basketball Book.* North Mankato, Minn.: Capstone Press, 2011.

INTERNET SITES

FactHound offers a safe, fun way to find Internet sites related to this book. All of the sites on FactHound have been researched by our staff.

Here's all you do:

Visit *www.facthound.com*

Type in this code: 9781491407417

Check out projects, games and lots more at
www.capstonekids.com

INDEX

Abdul-Jabbar, Kareem, 10, 11, 26
Archibald, Nate "Tiny", 28, 29

Boston Celtics, 16, 28
Bryant, Kobe, 24, 25

Chamberlain, Wilt, 6, 7, 8, 18, 29
Chicago Bulls, 14, 15, 23
Curry, Dell, 8
Curry, Seth, 9
Curry, Stephen, 8, 9

Hardaway, Tim, 26, 27

Jackson, Phil, 22, 23
Jordan, Michael, 14, 15, 18, 20, 21

Los Angeles Lakers, 16, 17, 23, 25

NBA Championships, 15, 16, 17, 25, 28

Pippen, Scottie, 14, 21

Robertson, Oscar, 12, 13
Rodman, Dennis, 14
Russell, Bill, 5

West, Jerry, 18, 19